BIOGRAPHIES

NARENDRA MODI

THE VISIONARY LEADER SHAPING INDIA'S TOMORROW

Manasvi Vohra

Published by:

V&S PUBLISHERS

F-2/16, Ansari Road, Daryaganj, New Delhi - 110002
☎ 23240026, 23240027 • *Fax:* 011-23240028
✉ info@vspublishers.com • 🌐 www.vspublishers.com

 **Online Brand Store: amazon.in/vspublishers**

Regional Office: Hyderabad
5-1-707/1, Brij Bhawan (Beside Central Bank of India Lane)
Bank Street, Koti, Hyderabad - 500 095
☎ 040-24737290
✉ vspublishershyd@gmail.com

Follow us on:   

BUY OUR BOOKS FROM: AMAZON FLIPKART

© Copyright: *V&S* PUBLISHERS
ISBN 978-81-978303-5-8
New Edition

Publisher's Note

Since the beginning of our operations in 2010, **V&S Publishers** has been devoted to bringing you one of the best and widest selections of books from across reading genres. Our work is defined by our very name, Value and Substance (V&S), which is at the heart of the books we publish. In becoming one of the leading publishers of general trade books in the mass-appeal genre in India, we have focused on developing a repertoire of titles that not just seek to inspire our readers to grow and flourish in life, but also spark a love for varied cultures and languages. Today, our catalogue has expanded to more than 1000 titles, across the categories of academic, children's stories, parenting, popular science, religion and spirituality, self-improvement, and many more.

Narendra Modi, the incumbent Prime Minister of India, has emerged as one of the most influential and controversial leaders in modern Indian history. His journey from the chief minister of Gujarat to the highest office of the largest democracy is a testimony to his political acumen, strategic vision and unwavering determination. This biography offers a detailed and balanced account of the life of a man whose vision and decisions continue to shape the future of India.

Through insightful analysis, this biography explores the personal and political dimensions of Modi's life, offering an in-depth understanding of his policies and the controversies that have surrounded his tenure. We believe that this biography will serve as an invaluable resource to understand the complexities of Narendra Modi's leadership and the broader perspective of his governance.

We sincerely hope our effort in bringing out this offering will be greeted by the warm and enthusiastic reception of our readers.

Contents

Childhood and Early Years

Narendra Damodardas Modi was born in a Hindu Gujarati family of grocers in Vadnagar, Bombay State (presently Gujarat), on September 17th, 1950. Narendra Modi's family traces their roots to the community of oil pressers, commonly known as *Modh Ghanchi Teli*.

Young Narendra was the third child among six children, born to Damodardas Mulchand Modi and Hiraben Modi. As described by his teachers, he was an average but dedicated student, who had a keen interest in debating and theatre. When he participated in theatrical productions in his youth, he had a proclivity for playing larger-than-life characters, which went on to influence his political imager later in life.

Prime Minister Narendra Modi with his mother

A dedicated workaholic, Narendra Modi never took a holiday or a sick day off during his 13 years serving as the Chief Minister of Gujarat.

As a young boy, he was exceptionally hard working and would help his father run the tea stall after school. At the age of eight, young Narendra joined the Rashtriya Swayamsewak Sangh (RSS), which is a Hindu nationalist volunteer paramilitary organisation.

(a) Teenage Narendra Modi in RSS Uniform

(b) Narendra Modi during his early years in RSS.

The Formative Years

Soon, young Narendra started attending the local *shakhas* (training sessions) organised by RSS. It was during his time here that he was introduced to Lakshmanrao Imandar, who was also known as Vakil Sahab. Lakshmanrao Imandar conferred the title of *Balswayamsevak* (junior cadet) on young Narendra. Thereafter, Inamdar became his mentor for many years to come and played an influential role in his life. While Modi was still training with RSS, he met Vasant Gajendragadkar and Nathalal Jaghda, who were leaders of Bhartiya Jana Sangha and went on to found the Gujarat unit of the Bhartiya Janata Party (BJP).

Narendra Modi and LakshmanRao Inamdar

A Timeline of Modi's Early Years

Year	Activities
1971	Worked as a full-time RSS worker
1980	Joined Bhartiya Jana Sangha

After completing his secondary education in northeastern Gujarat, Modi was married off to Jashodaben Chimanlal at the age of 18. However, he left his wife within a few months of his marriage. Reportedly, he left his wife without officially divorcing her, and their marriage was never consummated. He had kept his marriage hidden, as it was necessary to become a *pracharak* (party worker) in the puritan set up of the RSS. Modi publicly acknowledged their relationship nearly four decades later, as required by the Indian law.

Early Political Phase

Even during his early years, Modi was a deeply religious person. After leaving his parental home, he travelled extensively in Northern India. During his travels, Modi visited many Hindu *asharams* founded by Swami Vivekananda. One of these *ashrams* was located near Belur Math on the outskirts of

Kolkata. He also journeyed to Advaita Asharams in Almora and the Ramakrishna Mission in Rajkot. It is said that Modi's early life was largely influenced by the ideas of Swami Vivekananda.

In mid-1968, Modi was eager to stay at Belur Math, but he was sent back. He then wandered through West Bengal and Assam, with stopovers in Siliguri and Guwahati. He attempted to visit Ramakrishna Ashram in Almora, but faced repeated rejections. In the late 1960s, he returned to Vadnagar briefly before leaving for Ahmedabad. During this period, he lived with one of his uncles and worked in his canteen at the Gujarat State Road Transport Corporation.

After experiencing rejections, Modi returned to Ahmedabad with the idea of rekindling his connection with Inamdar. At that time, Inamdar was working at Hedgevar Bhawan, the RSS headquarters in the city. It was in 1971 that marked Modi's first foray into political activity as an adult. During the Bangladesh Liberation War in 1971, he joined Bhartiya Jana Sangh in Delhi, at the time led by late Shri Atal Bihari Vajpayee.

*Shri Narendra Modi with prominent
Bhartiya Jan Sangh leader Shri Atal Bihari Vajpayee*

His open support for the Mukti Bahini led to criticism from the India Gandhi-led government and he was briefly imprisoned in Tihar Jail. According to Modi, he was arrested during a non-violent protest against the government in New Delhi, just before Bangladesh Liberation War broke out. This event prompted Inamdar to mentor him for a few years. In the same year, Modi left his uncle's canteen to become a full-time *pracharak* for the RSS by joining hands with Inamdar. Years later, Modi co-authored a biography of Inamdar, which was published in 2001.

Academic Journey

Modi pursued his Bachelor of Arts degree in Political Science from Delhi University in 1978 through the School of Open Learning. He graduated with third-division grades. He then continued his education at Gujarat University, earning a Master of Arts degree with first-division grades. He was able to pursue his master's degree through distance learning over five years.

<table><tr><td>A Hidden Passion for Poetry and Photography</td></tr><tr><td>Not many people know that Narendra Modi enjoys writing poems and engaging in photography. He likes to write poems in Gujarati and has also authored several books. His impressive collection of photographs has been displayed in exhibitions.</td></tr></table>

That said, Modi's educational qualifications have drawn some scrutiny. Questions have arisen due to the absence of records of students receiving a graduation degree in 1978 from the School of Open Learning. This has been a topic of discussion among leaders of other political parties. However, it is important to note that no substantiated claims have emerged so far.

Sources:

https://en.wikipedia.org/wiki/Narendra_Modi#Early_political_career

https://www.britannica.com/biography/Narendra-Modi

https://www.theceo.in/leaders/narendra-modi-birthday-special-some-unknown-facts-about-narendra-modi-you-dont-know

2

Early Political Career

In early June 1975, the then Prime Minister of India, Ms. Indira Gandhi, declared a State of Emergency that lasted until 1977. During this period, many political leaders were jailed and several political groups were outlawed.

The State of Emergency

At this time, Narendra Modi served as a general secretary for an RSS committee called "Gujarat Lok Sangharsh Samiti." However, when the RSS was also banned, Modi had to go into hiding, moving from place to place to avoid arrest. During this time, he engaged in various activities, such as printing pamphlets and protesting the actions of the government. He also organised many rallies and demonstrations.

First Prime Minister in Independent India
Narendra Modi is the first Prime Minister to have been born in Independent India.

Additionally, Modi gained popularity amongst the vilified communities by establishing secure shelters and raising funds for those who were wanted by the government and political activists. During this period, he authored a book in Gujarati, titled *Sangharsh Ma Gujarat*, describing the State of Emergency and related events. In addition to going underground, Modi also disguised himself as a Sikh while travelling in Gujarat during Emergency. At this time, he notably interacted with influential political figures, including the renowned socialist leader, George Fernandes, who went on to support his political journey.

Book written by Narendra Modi during the 1975 emergency

Climbing the Ranks in RSS

In 1978, Modi advanced his political career by becoming an RSS *sambhag pracharak* (regional organizer). He actively managed political activities in parts of Surat and Vadodara. In 1979, he relocated to Delhi where he was assigned the task of researching the RSS's history of the Emergency.

In 1985, Modi underwent a significant shift, when he joined the BJP on the recommendation of the RSS. He successfully spearheaded several BJP election campaigns in Ahmedabad, contributing to the party's victory on a narrow margin. His performance in these elections earned him recognition, leading to his appointment for the post of "Organising Secretary" of the Gujarat division of BJP, in 1987. During this time, the BJP was under the presidency of Mr. LK Advani.

Modi made significant contributions during his foundational years in the BJP, becoming a member of the National Election Committee in 1990. He advanced within the party, lending a helping hand to organise the *Ram Rath Yatra*, which was led by LK Advani. He also actively participated in coordinating the *Ekta Yatra* in 1991–1992 alongside Murli Manohar Joshi.

Narendra Modi with prominent BJP leader, L.K. Advani

A Hiatus and Then a Return

After working rigorously over the years, Modi took a hiatus from his political career in 1992 that decided to establish a school in Ahmedabad. He dedicatedly worked towards this end for two years. However, in 1994, he returned to his electoral politics, persuaded by LK Advani.

In the 1995 state assembly elections, Modi's electoral strategies and superior political planning were credited for the BJP's victory. In November 1995, he was elected and appointed as the National Secretary of the BJP and relocated to Delhi. From there, he oversaw political activities in Haryana and Himachal Pradesh.

Chronicling Modi's Early Political Career

Year	Achievements
1975–1977	Appointed as the General Secretary of Gujarat Lok Sangharsh Committee
1975	RSS banned during the emergency
1975–1977	Organised safe homes and shelters for refugees and activists
1978	Published *Sangharsh Ma Gujarat*
Late 1970s	Met George Fernandes
1978	Becomes an RSS *Sambhag Pracharak*
1979	Moved to Delhi
1987	Appointed as Organising Secretary in the BJP by RSS
1990	Becomes member of National Election Committee
1990	Organised *Ram Rath Yatra*
1991–1992	Organised *Ekta Yatra*
1992–1994	Break from political career; worked towards establishing a school
1994	Returns to politics and becomes Party Secretary of the BJP

Sources:

https://en.wikipedia.org/wiki/Narendra_Modi#Early_political_career

https://www.britannica.com/biography/Narendra-Modi

https://edition.cnn.com/2015/01/19/world/narendra-modi-fast-facts/index.html

3

Gujarat's Visionary Chief Minister

By 2001, Mr. Keshubhai Patel – who was the then Chief Minister of Gujarat – fell ill. His health issues led to BJP's declining performance in the state assembly by-elections. There election results were marred by allegations of corruption, abuse of power, poor administration, and bribery, severely damaging Patel's standing.

Stepping into Leadership as Gujarat's Chief Minister

Further criticism arose after the fateful Bhuj Earthquake in 2001. Patel's handling of the natural disaster was criticised on all fronts. All these events led the BJP to seek a new candidate for chief ministership. Modi was selected to replace Keshubhai Patel, despite concerns from LK Advani about his level of experience. Modi, when offered the position of Deputy Chief Minister, declined it and told Atal Bihari Vajpayee and L.K Advani that he would either accept full responsibility or nothing.

On 3rd October 2001, Modi finally assumed office as the Chief Minister of Gujarat. He was sworn in as the Chief Minister of Gujarat on October 7th, 2001. With this post, he was given the responsibility to prepare the BJP for the upcoming elections in December 2002.

After winning a by-election in Rajkot constituency, Modi entered the Gujarat legislature on 24th February 2002. In these elections, he defeated Ashwin Mehta of the Indian National Congress.

A Dark Chapter: The 2002 Gujarat Riots

Soon after the by-election results, the riots erupted in Gujarat. On 27th February 2002, a train carrying over 500 passengers was tragically set on fire near Godhra. It resulted in the death of around 60 passengers. This train was on a pilgrimage route, ferrying devotees returning from Ayodhya, where they had attended a religious ceremony at the site of the demolished Babri Masjid. In a public statement, Modi described this incident as a pre-planned terrorist attack attributed to Muslims.

On 28th February, the day following the Godhra massacre, the Vishwa Hindu Parishad (VHP) called for a *bandh* (strike) across the state. During the *bandh*, severe riots erupted between Muslims and Hindus, sparking anti-Muslim violence across Gujarat. When the government decided to transport the bodies of the train victims from Godhra to Ahmedabad, it further fuelled violence and hatred.

Few months later, the government reported that approximately 800 Muslims and 280 Hindus had been killed during the Gujarat riots. Independent sources suggested a higher death toll, possibly reaching 2000, with the majority being Muslims. Many refugee camps were established, accommodating more than 1,50,000 people, including women and children who experienced violence on an unprecedented scale.

The Government of Gujarat faced substantial criticism for its poor management and administrative response during Gujarat riots. However, the Modi government decided to impose curfew in more than 26 major cities and issue strict shoot-at-sight orders. Patrolling units were deployed to monitor road violence, but these efforts proved ineffective as the situation remained uncontrolled. The refugee camps organised for the victims did not meet their daily needs. But the state officials urged the people to stay despite the challenges.

In yet another controversial incident, Muslims victims faced further discrimination when the government initially announced that their compensation would be half of what was given to Hindu victims. This decision was challenged in the court by the Muslim community, and the offer was withdrawn. It was also later revealed that some police officers willingly did not intervene in the riot situation.

The personal involvement of Modi in these 2002 Gujarat Riots remains a subject of debate. At the time of the riots, he remarked that "…whatever is happening is a chain of action and reactions." In a later interview, he regretted over how he handled the media.

In March 2008, a Special Investigation Team (SIT) was appointed by Supreme Court to re-examine cases related to the Gujarat Riots, including the Gulbarg Society Massacre. Following the petitions, in March 2010, the Supreme Court summoned Modi for questioning. In May, all reports were submitted proving, showing no evidence of Modi's complicity.

In July 2011, the court appointed Raju Ramachandran to submit the final report regarding the matter. Contrary to SIT'S findings, Ramachandran suggested that Modi could be proven guilty based on the available evidence. The case was then transferred from the Supreme Court to the Magistrate Court. Ramchandran's report was closely examined by SIT and submitted for final drafting in March 2012. The case was recommended to be closed.

Continuing Leadership: Modi's Later Terms

The aftermath of the riots brought significant criticism to Modi. There was widespread anger and condemnation, within and outside Gujarat, with many calling for Modi's resignation as Chief Minister. In April 2002, Modi officially submitted his resignation during the BJP national executive meeting in Goa, but it was not accepted. The Election Commissioner expressed concerns about the displaced voters and the prevailing situation.

Despite opposition, Modi successfully moved forward with elections in December 2002. The BJP had a significant victory in these elections, winning 127 out of 182 seats in the state assembly. Modi strategically secured a two-thirds majority (127 out of 182 seats) in the state assembly, defeating Yatin Oza of the Indian National Congress in the Maninagar constituency. He was sworn in for his second term in December 2002.

As his second term began, the focus of the government shifted from Hindutva to Gujarat's economic development. Modi was influenced by various organisations, including the Sangh Parivar, Bhartiya Kisan Sangh (BKS), and Vishwa Hindu Parishad (VHP). Over time, Modi re-established his connections with some of the Hindu nationalists. In 2014, he wrote a foreword to a textbook by Dinanath Batra, the former General Secretary of Vidya Bharti – a school network run by RSS.

Certain instances indicate that Modi's relationship with Muslims continued to face criticism. Ahead of the 2004 Lok Sabha elections, Prime Minister Atal Bihari Vajpayee distanced himself from the controversies and sought to reach out to the Muslims in North India. Vajpayee also strongly opposed Modi continuing his tenure in office after the riots, blaming him for the BJP's electoral defeat.

A number of Western nations also questioned Modi's relationship with Muslims. He became the only person who was denied a US visa under the International Religious Freedom. After acknowledging his role during the Gujarat riots, the UK government and the European Union refused to admit him to their countries. However, in 2012 and 2013, the UK government and EU lifted their bans, respectively. Later, in 2014, when Modi became the prime minster of India, the US also eased the ban and invited him to Washington D.C.

Modi's repeated success in Gujarat cemented his position as an indispensable leader of the BJP, ultimately leading to his reintegration. In July 2007, Modi became the longest-serving Chief Minister of Gujarat, having completed 2063 consecutive days in office. In the state elections that year, the BJP won 122 out of 182 seats. During this time, he built a formidable reputation for boosting the state's economy significantly, earning widespread appreciation.

Modi's election campaigns often featured elements of Hindu nationalism, evident in the 2007 and 2012 elections. He actively participated in Hindu religious ceremonies and developed relationships with Hindu religious leaders. In the 2012 elections, there were instances where he declined to wear clothes gifted by Muslim leaders, even though he maintained good relations with the Dawoodi Bohra community.

In the 2012 elections, Modi employed a strategy that identified himself with the state of Gujarat, similar to Indira Gandhi's approach during the Emergency, portraying himself as the guardian of Gujarat against prosecution by the rest of India. To reach a larger audience, he used advanced technologies, like holograms.

In the subsequent campaign in 2014, Modi employed similar strategies and defeated Shweta Bhatt, an Indian National Congress candidate, to win the Maninagar constituency. Upon becoming Prime Minister, Modi resigned as Chief Minister of Gujarat, and Anandiben Patel, the MLA from Maninagar, succeeded him as Chief Minister.

A Vision for Progress

During his tenure as Chief Minister, Modi advocated for a small government and supported privatisation, a departure from RSS ideology, which favoured anti-privatisation and anti-globalisation policies. His approach aimed to reduce corruption in the state. He worked tirelessly to establish financial and technology parks in Gujarat, with the 2007 Vibrant Gujarat Summit witnessing real estate investment deals worth 6.6 trillion.

Modi and Patel collaborated to support various NGOs and communities in building groundwater conservation projects. By December 2008, over 500,000 structures were constructed for ground water conservation projects, including 11,378 check dams to recharge aquifers. By 2010, they successfully restored 60 of the 112 *tehsils* that had depleted water tables since 2004. This restoration led to significant improvements in the production of genetically modified cotton in Gujarat, making India the largest producer.

Consequently, Gujarat's agriculture sector saw remarkable growth, with a 9.6 per cent increase from 2001 to 2007. Some of the lesser successful projects included public irrigation measures in parts of central and southern Gujarat and the installation of Sardar Sarovar Dam. The Sardar Sarovar project was successful in irrigating only 4 to 6 per cent of the allotted area.

Modi made yet another strategic move by offering land in Gujarat to Tata Motors for their Nano automobile plant, which attracted several other companies to the state.

Under Modi's leadership, the government completed the electrification of every village in Gujarat, including remote areas. His efforts to revamp the power distribution system had a significant positive impact on farmers.

One notable initiative was the introduction and expansion of the Jyotigram Yojna, which separated agricultural electricity from rural electricity. This move substantially reduced the cost of agricultural electricity as it was allocated to meet scheduled irrigation demands. This change resolved protests by farmers who had previously faced electricity supply issues in their areas, benefiting them and stabilising their power supplies.

Controversies and Discourses: The Development Agenda

Gujarat's economic development during Modi's tenure as chief minister sparked continuous debates and discussions. The state experienced an average GDP growth of nearly 10 per cent, surpassing other industrialized states and the national average.

However, it is important to note that economic growth in the 1990s, before Modi's tenure, was also relatively high. Modi facilitated Special Economic Zones, which relaxed labour laws to attract investment.

<table>
<tr><td>Taking Gujarat to New Heights</td></tr>
<tr><td>Under Modi's guidance, Gujarat gained recognition for its business-friendly environment, topping global rankings for two consecutive years. In 2013, the state was ranked first in India for economic freedom, considering factors like growth, governance, citizens' rights, labour flexibility, and business regulations.</td></tr>
</table>

Despite steady economic growth, Gujarat faced challenges in areas such as human development, poverty alleviation, nutrition, and education during Modi's tenure. In 2013, the state ranked 13th in the country for poverty and 21st for education. Gujarat was placed in a concerning category on the India State Hunger Index, with data indicating that nearly 45 per cent of children were underweight and over 23 per cent were undernourished.

From 2001 to 2011, Gujarat showed little improvement in terms of female literacy and poverty, keeping it close to the median among the 29 Indian states. While there was a slight reduction in infant mortality rates, the quality of education in both government and private schools in Gujarat lagged behind. Despite the launch of various social policies by the Modi government, many segments of society, including Muslims, Dalits, and Adivasis, did not benefit, leading to social inequalities within the region.

Development appeared to primarily benefit the urban middle class, leaving weaker sections of society lacking essential services. In 2013, the Modi government ranked 10th out of 21 states in the Human Development Index, indicating room for improvement.

❐❐❐

4

The Road to Prime Ministership

Modi's nomination for the position of Prime Minister by the BJP in the 2014 Lok Sabha Elections took place in September 2013. However, his candidacy faced opposition from many BJP leaders who sought to cancel his nomination. LK Advani expressed concerns and supported other party leaders in opposing Modi's candidacy. Despite this internal dissent, Modi played a central role in all election campaigns. Many people strongly supported him, considering Modi the driving force behind the BJP's electoral prospects.

Landmark Victory: General Elections in 2014
During his election campaigns for the BJP, Modi raised his voice against the corruption scandals of the time and presented himself as a politician capable of boosting the state's GDP. His messages resonated with younger generation and the middle class. Modi worked diligently to address criticism related to secularism and sought to improve protection measures for religious minority groups.

Before the elections, Modi was often portrayed as a controversial figure due to his role in the Gujarat riots. However, following the BJP's victory, he received recognition for his neoliberal policies and was credited as a key figure behind Gujarat's development. While the campaign focused on Hindutva, communal tensions arose, particularly in Uttar Pradesh and parts of Northeast India.

The media played a significant role in supporting the BJP's election campaigns. The estimated cost of Modi's election campaign was approximately 50 billion rupees. In addition to traditional campaign methods, Modi extensively utilised social media platforms to connect with the public. He addressed over 1000 rallies through hologram appearances!

Following the election campaigns, the BJP secured 31 per cent of the votes, more than doubling its Lok Sabha tally to 282 seats. This victory marked the first time since 1984 that a single party had won a majority independently. Dissatisfaction with the INC and other political parties drove voters to support the BJP. The RSS strongly supported the BJP, and the party performed exceptionally well in states like Uttar Pradesh, where it received significant support from upper-caste Hindus, as well as over 10 per cent of the Muslim vote.

The BJP's success in areas with recent Hindu-Muslim violence led many commentators to believe that the election had shifted away from progressive parties and leaned towards right-wing politics. Modi's tweets about his victory reflected this shift, emphasising capitalism and Hindu cultural nationalism over secular and social tactics.

Depicting Narendra Modi's victory in 2014 Lok Sabha Elections

Renewed Mandate: General Elections in 2019

On 13th October 2018, Modi was announced as the BJP candidate for the position of Prime Minister. Amit Shah played a central role in leading the election campaign. In response to the INC's campaign titled "Chowkidar Chor Hai" (The Watchman is a Thief), Modi launched the "Main Bhi Chowkidar" (I am also a Watchman) campaign in the run-up to the 2019 general elections. In mid-2018, the Telugu Desam Party split from the NDA (National Democratic Alliance) due to issues related to special status for Andhra Pradesh.

The Story Behind "Chowkidaar"

The literal meaning of the word *chowkidaar* is "watchman." During the 2014 election campaigns, Narendra Modi promised that he would safeguard his country not only as the Prime Minister of India, but also as a watchman. He specifically referred to himself as a *chowkidaar* because he made it clear that he wouldn't tolerate any corruption in the country. He emphasised that, in his role as a watchman, he would prevent anyone from misusing public funds.

Chowkidaar Chor Hai vs Main Bhi Chowkidaar

Chowkidaar chor hai meaning *The watchman is a thief* was a slogan used by Rahul Gandhi during the 2019 General Elections. It was coined by the INC to accuse Narendra Modi of corruption and misconduct in the Dassault Rafale Deal. Rahul Gandhi used this slogan to convey to the public that the person responsible for safeguarding their money (the watchman) was, in fact, a thief.

On 14th March 2019, Modi responded to Rahul Gandhi's slogan by stating, *Main bhi Chowkidar*, which translates to *I Too Am a Watchman*. Modi used this response to imply that he is a vigilant protector and not a coward. He pledged to fight against corruption and social evils in the country with full force. To support this slogan, he even changed his X handle from "Narendra Modi" to "*Chowkidaar* Narendra Modi."

In a coordinated campaign, Amit Shah and many other political leaders from the BJP actively supported Modi by adding the prefix *Chowkidaar* to their names on Twitter (now known as X). Modi also addressed large groups of watchmen to garner their support for his campaign. To counter Modi's campaign, INC supporters changed their X handles to *"Main bhi Berozgaar,"* meaning *"I am also unemployed,"* to highlight the rising unemployment issues during Modi's tenure.

Electoral Triumph and International Relations

Modi tirelessly focused on ensuring national security and made defence a central topic of national interest during his election campaigns. One of the greatest achievements of his administration came in response to the Pulwama attack, with the retaliatory Balakot airstrike.

In his election campaigns, Modi also emphasised crucial issues, such as developing and fostering strong foreign relationships.

During the Lok Sabha elections, Modi contested from Varanasi. As expected, he secured a resounding victory by defeating Shalini Yadav, the candidate from Samajwadi Party (SP), with a margin of 479,505 votes.

Following this victory, the NDA unanimously appointed Modi as the Prime Minister for the second time. Out of the total 352 seats, BJP won an overwhelming 303 seats, solidifying their dominance.

Sources:

https://en.wikipedia.org/wiki/Narendra_Modi#Premiership_campaigns
https://en.wikipedia.org/wiki/Main_Bhi_Chowkidar
https://en.wikipedia.org/wiki/Chowkidar_Chor_Hai

5

Leading India as Prime Minister

On 26th May 2014, Narendra Modi was inaugurated as the Prime Minister of India, following the significant victory of the BJP-led National Democratic Alliance (NDA) in the 2014 Lok Sabha elections. This marked a historic moment as he became the first Prime Minister of India born after the country gained independence from the British Empire in 1947.

In 2019, when the NDA secured victory once again, Narendra Modi was reappointed as Prime Minister for a second term. On 6th December 2020, he achieved the distinction of becoming the fourth longest-serving Prime Minister in India's history and the longest-serving non-Congress Prime Minister.

Modi took his oath as the Prime Minister of India in two separate ceremonies. In the first term, he was sworn in the presence of India's then-President Pranab Mukherjee, who administered the oath. During his second term, the oath was administered by India's President at that time, Ram Nath Kovind.

PM, Narendra Modi and incumbent President Draupadi Murmu

Governance and Other Initiatives

During Modi's first year as Prime Minister, there was a significant centralisation of powers. The Rajya Sabha, as the upper house of the Indian Parliament, required a majority of votes from the BJP. Initially, the BJP lacked the seats in the Rajya Sabha, but Modi managed to pass many ordinances to implement his policies, furthering his interest in centralising power.

Illustration depicting Narendra Modi answering a question in the Lok Sabha

Throughout his administration, he modified the bill to increase his control over the selection and appointment of judges, which significantly reduced the role of the judiciary.

In December 2014, he made a major change by abolishing the Planning Commission and replacing it with the renowned NITI Aayog (National Institution for Transforming India).

NITI Aayog
NITI Aayog, formed in 2015 by the Indian Government, replaced the Planning Commission, which used to follow a top-down approach. It acts as a public policy think tank, focusing on economic development and cooperative federalism by engaging State Governments in a bottom-up approach. Key initiatives include a 15-year road map, a 7-year vision strategy, and reforms in areas such as agriculture, medical education, and innovation under the Atal Innovation Mission and Digital India.

The Planning Commission, formerly responsible for social justice, faced severe criticism for its ineffectiveness in improving social welfare.

In his first year, Modi initiated investigations by the Intelligence Bureau into various civil society and foreign non-governmental organisations. These probes revealed that some NGOs were hindering economic growth. Organisations, such as Médecins Sans Frontières, Sierra Club, and Avaaz, came under scrutiny. Sedition and terrorism charges were filed against individuals critical of the government, leading to comparisons with the Indira Gandhi-led government in the past.

Surprisingly, in his first three years, Modi abolished 1,200 outdated laws. He introduced the concept of Digital India, promoting electronic government services. He expanded high-speed Internet access, fostering digital literacy and boosting domestic electronic production.

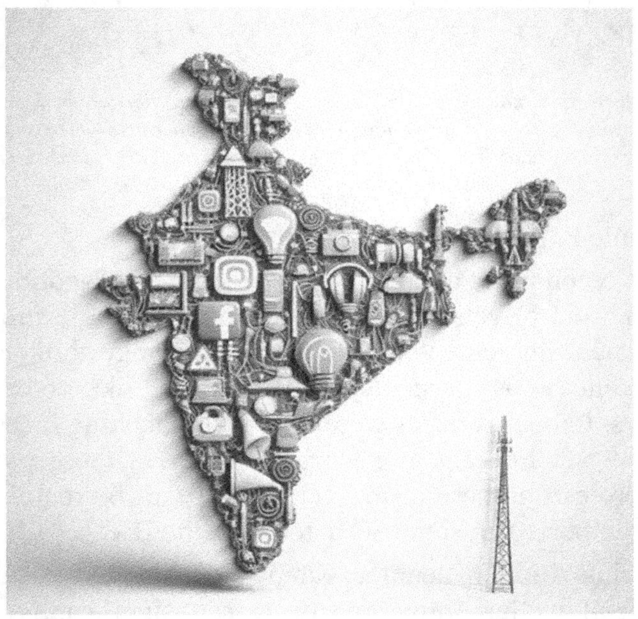

An AI generated illustration made of symbols which stand for connectivity which is the aim of Digital India

In the year 2015, under the leadership of Modi, India celebrated the first for the first time, International Yoga Day on June 21, 2015. The Ujjwala scheme introduced in 2019 for government jobs and education. The Ujjwala Scheme in 2016 provided free LPG connections to rural communities, increasing LPG access by 24 per cent in 2019. Modi also earned favour among the economically disadvantaged by passing a 10 per cent reservation law in 2019 for government jobs and education.

(a) Illustration showing Narendra Modi practising Yoga on International Yoga Day near India Gate

(b) AI illustration capturing smiles on face of numerous women on getting subsidized LPG cylinders under Ujjwala Scheme

Economic Policy

Modi's economic approach was rooted in Neoliberalism, focusing on privatisation and economic liberalisation. His government implemented policies to encourage foreign direct investment (FDI), particularly in industries like defence and railways. Labour reforms were introduced, making it easier for employers to hire and fire workers. Some of these proposals faced protests and criticism, including strikes by major unions in September 2015, some affiliated with the BJP.

During Modi's tenure, funding for poverty reduction and social welfare programs decreased significantly. While Congress allocated 14.6 per cent of GDP to social programs, this dropped to 12.6 per cent during Modi's tenure. Corporate taxes were reduced; wealth tax was eliminated; sales tax was increased; and customs duties on gold and jewellery were reduced. Diesel prices were de-regulated in 2014.

Education spending as a share of the budget decreased from 0.7 per cent to 0.5 per cent over five years. Funding for children's health, nutrition, and education programs was also halved between 2014 and 2022. However, capital investment in transport infrastructure increased from 0.7 per cent in 2014 to 1.7 per cent in 2022.

Modi launched the Make in India initiative in 2014 to encourage foreign companies to manufacture their products in India, aiming to make the country a global manufacturing hub. However, critics feared foreign dominance in the Indian market. Modi introduced a land reform bill allowing private ownership of agricultural land without social impact assessments or farmers' consent. It lapsed due to opposition in Parliament. The Goods and Services Tax (GST), effective from 1st July 2017, was a major tax reform, consolidating 17 different taxes.

To address issues of black money, counterfeit currency, corruption, and terrorism, Modi's government demonetised Rs. 500 and 1000 banknotes, causing cash shortages, stock market declines, and job losses. The move led to a 1 per cent reduction in India's GDP and 1.5 million job losses. But it boosted digital transactions and increased individual income tax returns by 25 per cent.

While Modi's tenure saw GDP growth, it also witnessed high unemployment levels, with the highest in 45 years due to demonetisation and the GST. In the 2019–2020 fiscal year, GDP growth slowed to 4.18 per cent with an inflation rate of 4.7 per cent. Despite challenges, Modi remained committed to his economic principles, aspiring to elevate India's economy further.

Health and Sanitation
During Modi's first term as Prime Minister, he reduced government spending on healthcare. In January 2015, he introduced the New Health Policy (NHP), which didn't increase government healthcare spending but instead highlighted the role of private health organisations. This

was a departure from the previous government's focus on healthcare programs to reduce child and maternal mortality, leading to a 20 per cent reduction in funds for programs like the National Health Mission in 2015.

In the second year of his administration, Modi continued to cut healthcare funds by 25 per cent. However, in the following year, the healthcare budget increased by 19 per cent, which was well received by private insurance providers.

Modi aimed to promote public sanitation for better health. On 2nd October 2015, he launched the Swachh Bharat Abhiyan (Clean India initiative) with a goal to eliminate public open defecation and manual scavenging within five years. Labourers and engineers were deployed to build toilets in rural areas and people were encouraged to use them. The government also focused on sewage treatment plants.

Modi's administration set a target of constructing 60 million toilets by the end of 2019. During this initiative, there were corruption allegations, and some people hesitated to use the new public toilets. Nonetheless, the sanitation coverage increased from 38.7 per cent in 2014 to 84.1 per cent in 2018. However, the usage of these facilities lagged in some areas.

Swachh Bharat Abhiyan

In 2014, Modi initiated the "One Step Toward Cleanliness" campaign with the goal of eradicating open defecation, improving solid waste management, and promoting menstrual health awareness. The Swachh Bharat Abhiyan was launched in two phases. Phase 1, which ran until October 2019, focused on eliminating manual scavenging, constructing rural toilets, changing sanitation practices, and expanding sanitation infrastructure. Phase 2, implemented between 2020–2021, aimed to accelerate the tasks from Phase 1. This mission, India's largest cleanliness drive, was inaugurated at Rajghat, New Delhi, and engaged over 5 million government employees and students nationwide in an effort to make India cleaner.

In March 2020, the Modi government invoked the Epidemic Disease Act of 1947 and the Disaster Management Act of 2005 in response to the COVID-19 pandemic. With COVID-19 cases on the rise, Modi suspended all commercial and international flights in March. Restrictions gradually eased in April and were completely lifted by the end of November 2020.

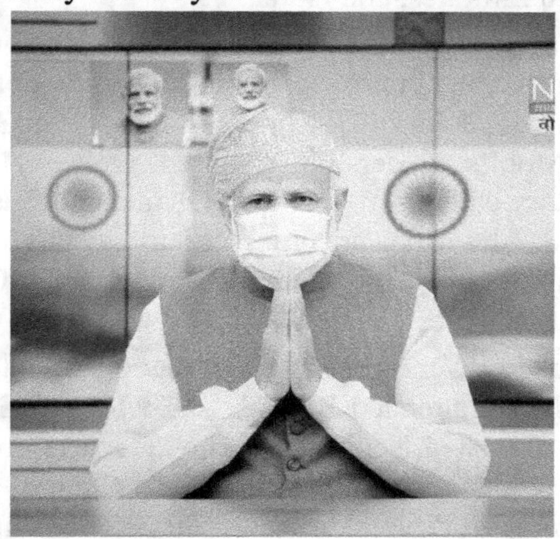

Prime Minister of India declaring the COVID 19 lockdown

The second COVID-19 wave proved more devastating than the first. The country faced shortages of oxygen, vaccines, ICU beds, hospital beds, and medical supplies during this time. In late April, India reported the world's highest number of cases. India initiated its vaccination drive in January 2021, administering 1.7 billion doses by January 2022, fully vaccinating nearly 720 million people.

Foreign Policy

During Modi's election campaign, foreign policy played a minor role, and the BJP's election manifesto provided limited evidence of foreign policies. Similar to the preceding Congress government, Modi's foreign policy focused on improving economic ties, security, and regional relations. He continued the policy of "multi-alignment," a concept initiated by Manmohan Singh.

Additionally, Modi launched initiatives like "Make in India" and "Digital India" to attract foreign investments, particularly from East Asian countries. Additionally, the government sought to strengthen ties with Middle Eastern Islamic nations, including Bahrain, Iran, Saudi Arabia, the United Arab Emirates, and Israel.

After becoming Prime Minister, India's relations with the United States also improved. Despite earlier concerns due to his visa denial in 2005 while serving as Gujarat's Chief Minister, Modi's leadership garnered praise. He received congratulatory calls from President Obama and was invited to visit the US. The Modi government successfully built strong foreign relations with the US under both Barack Obama and Donald Trump's presidencies.

Modi made several trips to different countries to fulfill his policy goals. He attended BRICS, ASEAN, and G20 summit meetings and visited Nepal, where he agreed to provide USD one billion in aid. His visits to the US, despite past visa issues, aimed to enhance diplomatic and trade relationships between the two countries.

Narendra Modi in an International Conference

In 2015, the Indian Parliament approved a land exchange deal with Bangladesh, originally initiated by Manmohan Singh. Modi renamed the "Look East Policy" to the "Act East Policy," redirecting India's foreign policy toward East Asia and Southeast Asia. He signed agreements to improve land connectivity with Myanmar, involving the state of Manipur. However, India's relationship with China deteriorated significantly after the 2020 India-China skirmish.

Modi also built stronger ties with Afghanistan, pledging 900 million dollars in aid and making two visits to the country. In 2016, he received the nation's highest civilian award for his policies and work. Furthermore, Modi developed a good rapport with Russian President Vladimir Putin as part of his global networking efforts.

Defence Policy

Under Modi's administration, India's nominal military spending saw a significant increase. However, when considered as a fraction of GDP and adjusted for inflation, the military budget declined during his tenure. A substantial portion of the military budget was allocated to personnel costs.

During the election campaign, Modi maintained a firm stance, promising to be "tough on Pakistan. On 29th September 2016, the Indian Army announced that it had conducted a surgical strike targeting launch pads in Azad Kashmir. Initially, Pakistan denied that any such strike occurred. In February 2019, India carried out air strikes against Pakistan to target a terrorist camp, but they did not significantly impact high-value targets. Cross-border shelling and military skirmishes also occurred, resulting in the loss of an Indian aircraft.

After Modi's victory in the 2019 Lok Sabha elections, he prioritised India's defence policies, with a particular focus on China and Pakistan. On 5th May 2020, there were aggressive confrontations between Chinese and Indian troops in several border areas, including near the Pangong Lake in Ladakh and Tibet Autonomous regions. Additional clashes were reported along the Line of Actual Control (LAC) in Ladakh. These clashes led to tensions and responses from both sides. Subsequent talks, both military and diplomatic, aimed to restore peace.

Modi's affinity for Russian leader Vladimir Putin is noteworthy. In December 2021, Modi signed an agreement with Putin to enhance military-technical cooperation with Russia. India also purchased the S-400 missile system from Russia, strengthening their ties. During the 2022 Russian invasion of Ukraine, Modi maintained a neutral stance and condemned Russia's actions. He initiated "Operation Ganga" to evacuate stranded Indians not only from Ukraine but also from neighbouring countries. This operation successfully evacuated 19,000 nationals.

Environmental Policy

When it came to reforming environmental policies, Modi renamed the cabinet as the "Ministry of Environment, Forest, and Climate Change" from the "Ministry of Environment and Forest." However, during his first budget, the funds allocated to the ministry were reduced by 50 per cent. The new ministry introduced new laws related to environmental protection and industrial activities. Modi's government also attempted to restructure the National Board for Wildlife by removing representatives from non-governmental organisations – a move that was rejected by the Supreme Court.

Additionally, the Modi-led government undertook projects to reduce the ministry's involvement in small mining projects and allow activities inside forested lands without seeking permission from tribal councils. They also lifted bans on industrial activities in highly polluted areas. These changes were welcomed by businessmen but criticised by environmentalists.

Modi actively encouraged investments in solar power through the launch of the International Solar Alliance initiative in 2015. He blamed developed countries for India's limited historical role in climate change. During the COP26 conference, Modi pledged to expand India's renewable energy capacity by targeting carbon neutrality by 2070. His efforts received applause from environmentalists and economists, as India is now the only economy that has met the Paris Agreement goals. Under Modi's leadership, India has achieved a 10 per cent ethanol blending rate, five months ahead of schedule.

The Rise of Hindutva

During the tenure of the Modi government, several Hindu nationalist organisations became increasingly active. They launched campaigns focusing on Hindu religious conversion programmes to counter "Love *Jihad*" and commemorating Nathuram Godse, who assassinated Mahatma Gandhi. Notably, the Home Minister and other government officials did not endorse these religious conversions.

Under Modi's leadership, the BJP's ties with RSS strengthened. RSS provided organisational support for BJP's electoral campaigns, and in return, Modi appointed RSS members to key government positions. RSS members were also increasingly appointed in educational institutions.

The Modi government made changes in government-approved Hindi textbooks and magazines, emphasising Modi's achievements, and presenting Indian society as harmonious, free from conflicts and inequality, while de-emphasising Jawaharlal Nehru.

In 2019, Modi passed a citizenship law allowing persecuted religious minorities (Hindus, Sikhs, Parsis, Jains, Buddhists, Christians) excluding Muslims, from Afghanistan, Bangladesh, and Pakistan a path to Indian citizenship. This religious criterion for citizenship led to global criticism and protests and was temporarily halted due to the 2019 COVID-19 pandemic. Subsequently, demonstrations and protests, including the Delhi Riots of 2020, erupted, primarily targeting Muslims by Hindu mobs.

<table>
<tr><td>Delhi Riots of 2020</td></tr>
<tr><td>Also known as the Northeast Delhi Riots, the Delhi Riots of 2020 resulted in bloodshed, property destruction, and numerous protests in the northeastern part of the capital city. Out of the 53 fatalities during these riots, two-thirds were Muslims who were either shot, subjected to repeated attacks, or set on fire. The casualties also included police officers and intelligence agents.</td></tr>
</table>

In 2019, the Supreme Court ruled that disputed land in Ayodhya should be handed over to a Hindu trust for the construction of a temple, while also instructing the government to allocate 5 acres of land to the Sunni Waqf Board for a mosque. On 5th August 2020, Modi visited Ayodhya to oversee the construction of the Hindu temple, becoming the first prime minister to visit Ram Janmabhoomi and Hanuman Garhi.

Upon returning to power after the 2019 elections, Modi took three significant actions long advocated by the RSS. First, on 1st August 2020, he made the practice of Triple *Talaq* illegal and punishable. Under his administration, Article 370 of the Indian Constitution, which granted autonomy to Jammu and Kashmir, was revoked, and the region was reorganised into two union territories: Jammu and Kashmir, and Ladakh. Until February 2021, these areas were under strict lockdown with suspended Internet services and restricted movement. Numerous political leaders and thousands of people were detained.

Sources:

https://en.wikipedia.org/wiki/Narendra_Modi#Prime_Minister

https://en.wikipedia.org/wiki/Foreign_policy_of_the_Narendra_Modi_government

https://en.wikipedia.org/wiki/Swachh_Bharat_Mission

6

Legacy and Public Perception

During Modi's tenure, he consistently enjoyed high approval ratings and garnered widespread public support. In popular opinion polls, he has been ranked as one of the greatest prime ministers in India's history. Serving as the 14th Prime Minister of India, Modi's image, personality, background, and policies have been subjects of public perception.

Modi began his public career as a Hindu nationalist with the RSS in the 1970s, eventually transitioning to its political arm, the BJP, in 1980. Modi demonstrated his exceptional skills in organising successful political campaigns, steadily rising through the party ranks in the 1990s in his home state of Gujarat.

During his 14-year tenure as Chief Minister of Gujarat from 2001 to 2014, Modi elicited mixed reactions from the public. He faced criticism for alleged bias during the Gujarat Riots. However, he was also lauded for driving economic development in the state and was dubbed a *Vikas Purush*, which literally translates to "a development-oriented man."

Since 2014, Modi has served as a strong Prime Minister of India. Despite criticism for announcing and changing policies within short timeframes, he remains one of the most influential politicians in Indian history. The BJP has successfully conducted its national and regional election campaigns, with Modi as its central figure. To cultivate his image among the people, Modi has utilised multimedia communication technology and public relations (PR) strategies, including social media, government media outlets, and carefully managed public appearances.

Global Recognition and Impact

In 2007, India Today named Narendra Modi the best chief minister based on nationwide surveys of Indian Chief Ministers. In 2012, he achieved global recognition by appearing on the front page of the Asian edition of *Time Magazine* and being included in the Time 100 List of the World's Most Influential People. Forbes ranked him as the 15th most powerful person in the world, and he became Asia's most followed leader on X.

A 2017 survey by the Pew Research Centre showed that Modi surpassed Rahul Gandhi in terms of popularity by 88 per cent, Sonia Gandhi by 57 per cent, and Arvind Kejriwal by 39 per cent. He was even featured in a *Time Magazine* article titled "India's Divider in Chief," written by novelist Aaatish Taseer.

Approval Ratings

Throughout his premiership, Modi consistently received high approval ratings. In a Pew Research Poll at the end of his first year in office, he achieved an overall rating of 87 per cent, with 67 per cent of respondents viewing him as "very favourable." An impressive 93 per cent approved of his governmental performance.

In his second year, his approval rating remained steady at around 74 per cent. By the end of his third year, he reached his highest approval rating, with 88 per cent of people considering him "highly favourable."

According to various renowned polls, surveys, and magazines, Modi is regarded as one of the most popular figures in the history of Indian politics.

Mastery of Media Engagement

Modi has always been appreciated for his adoption of innovative communication strategies to connect with the people of India. This penchant for effective communication dates to his tenure as the Chief Minister of Gujarat. His efforts to enhance his image have encompassed a range of strategies, from donning various attires to leveraging social media platforms. These tactics have proven highly beneficial, particularly during his election campaigns.

As the Prime Minister of India, Modi ensured his presence was felt throughout the country through billboards, newspapers, magazines, TV advertisements, and even vaccine certificates. During his campaign speeches, Modi has at times adopted a messianic tone, suggesting that he derives his leadership qualities from a higher power.

Prime minister interacting with the masses through live telecasting on television

Narendra Modi extensively utilised social media as a direct means of communication with the public. By September 2014, he had amassed 5 million X followers. He introduced innovative strategies like live chats, making him the first political leader to engage with people through video conferencing and calls.

Critics have questioned Modi's communication strategies, particularly his heavy reliance on social media at the expense of traditional media channels, such as television and print. He has become less inclined to grant interviews and hold press conferences since coming to power in 2014. Instead, he has adopted a monthly monologue format known as Mann ki Baat, which airs on the government-owned All India Radio and Doordarshan. Supporters of Modi have applauded his efforts to connect with the public various mediums of mass communication. He uses them to promote positive social causes and engage in interactive sessions.

Modi's Persona

Narendra Modi hails from a family of vegetarians who abstained from alcohol. His lifestyle has always been frugal, and he is known for his strong work ethic and introverted nature. Since 2002, Badri Meena has served as his cook. Modi has been noted for his close and affectionate relationship with his mother, late Smt. Hiraben. He made history on 31st August 2012, by becoming the first Indian prime minister to engage in a live chat with citizens.

Scholars and biographers often describe Modi as highly influential, charismatic, bold, and energetic. In his 2008 book *Jyotipunj*, Modi profiles various RSS leaders he worked with, including MS Golwalkar, whom he reveres as *pujniya shri guruji* (Guru worthy of worship). With this book, Modi aimed to shed light on the work and principles of the RSS and reassure his RSS associates of his enduring ideological alignment with them. In addition, Modi has authored eight other books, primarily featuring short moral stories for children.

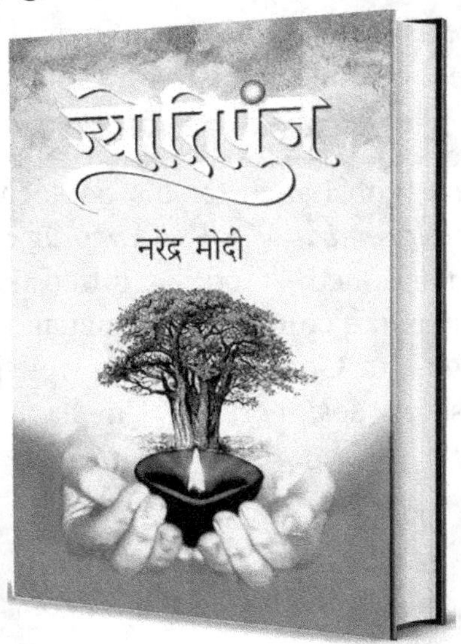

Jyotipunj: A book written by Narendra Modi

Modi has been described as one of the most contemporary, controversial, and divisive figures in Indian politics. During the 2014 general election campaign, the BJP portrayed Modi as a strong, bold, and independent leader capable of acting decisively in challenging times.

Sartorial Choices: A Visual Statement

Modi has always been quite eclectic when it comes to choosing his attire for different occasions, using clothing as a means of making visual statements. He often dresses to portray an image as the protector of Hindu India, as seen when he wore saffron-coloured outfits during the foundation stone ceremony at Ayodhya and other Hindu religious ceremonies.

Modi's clothing choices have sparked international discussions, earning him the title of a fashion-conscious political leader in India. His vests, in particular, became popular and were dubbed "Modi jackets," not only in India but also in several parts of the world. Typically, he prefers a *kurta* and a jacket. His choice of colours evolved from bright and bold during his tenure as Chief Minister of Gujarat to pastel colours when he became the Prime Minister of India.

A Unique Sense of Style

In an interview with Lance for his book titled *The Modi Effect: Inside Narendra Modi's Campaign to Transform India*, Modi mentioned, "God has gifted me the sense of mixing and matching colours. So, I manage everything on my own. Since I'm God-gifted, I fit well in everything. I have no fashion designer, but I'm happy to hear that I dress well."

(a) Narendra Modi in a unique avatar as he visits a tiger reserve

(b) New look adopted Narendra Modi during West Bengal Election campaigns in 2021

However, his fashion choices haven't been without controversy. During Barack Obama's state visit to Hyderabad House in 2015, Modi wore a suit with his name embroidered in the pinstripes, drawing criticism for the apparent contradiction between his humble background as the son of a tea seller and his luxury attire. The suit was later auctioned for US $695,000, with the proceeds donated to the mission to clean the Ganga.

Modi's clothing choices have always been a topic of discussion, with some describing his dressing style as "100% Indian," according to Vogue India's editor Priya Tanna.

During his tenure as the Chief Minister of Gujarat, Modi received many gifts. He chose to auction these gifts, raising Rs. 899.6 million. The proceeds from these auctions were donated to the Kanaya Kelavani fund to support girls' education, clean Ganga missions, and the welfare of underprivileged sections of society.

Cultural Depictions of Modi

Previously, in 2014, an Indian docudrama called *7 RCR* (7, Race Course Road) showcased the political careers of prominent Indian leaders, including Modi. However, the first biopic about Modi, titled *Modi Kaka Ka Gaon* (Modi Uncle's Town), was released in 2017. This Hindi-language drama, written by Tushar Amrish Goel, featured Vikas Mahante in the titular role. Another biographical drama, simply named *Narendra Modi*, was released in 2019 with Vivek Oberoi portraying Modi. It depicted Modi's journey to the prime ministership.

Another documentary titled *India: The Modi Question* faced criticism for its coverage of Modi's role during the Gujarat riots and his track record as Prime Minister.

In an effort to maintain his "hero-like" image, Modi appeared on the show *Man vs. Wild* on the Discovery Channel, becoming the second world leader after Barack Obama to participate in a live show. During the episode, he trekked through various jungles and discussed wildlife conservation with the host, Bear Grylls. The episode featuring Modi was filmed in Jim Corbett National Park, Uttarakhand, and was broadcasted in over 180 countries, including India.

Narendra Modi with Bear Grylls in the show Man Vs. Wild

Furthermore, Modi initiated *Pariksha Par Charcha*, which is an initiative aimed at discussing competitions and academic issues with students to improve India's educational system.

Modi interacting with school children

Challenges and Controversies

For many years, Modi was ostracised due to his alleged role in the Gujarat Riots, where he was accused of creating divisions between Hindus and Muslims. Consequently, he faced foreign visa bans from the US and several other countries. However, these restrictions were lifted before he assumed the position of Prime Minister of India. He subsequently developed positive foreign relations with Russia and European nations too.

Modi actively cultivated an image as a development-focused leader and aimed to make his state conducive for new business ventures. Known for his meticulous approach to governance, Modi began to face criticism in 2016 when he introduced demonetisation, causing widespread job losses and distress among people who relied heavily on cash.

In March 2020, Modi imposed a sudden nationwide lockdown in response to the surging COVID-19 cases, leading to loss of lives and widespread unemployment. This decision resulted in a significant contraction of the Indian economy.

Amidst the onset of the COVID-19 pandemic in March 2020, Modi established the PM CARES Fund, with senior cabinet colleagues and ministers of defence, home, and finance serving as trustees. In December 2020, the government declared it a public fund but did not disclose information under the Right to Information Act of 2005. Modi faced criticism for his perceived absence during the second wave of COVID-19 in April 2021, with observers noting his withdrawal during times of crisis.

While India has a parliamentary democracy, Modi often made unilateral decisions, bypassing input from both houses of Parliament. In September 2020, controversial farm reform laws were passed, leading to widespread protests. After a year of protests, Modi repealed the laws in November 2021 with minimal discussion in both the Lok Sabha and Rajya Sabha, sparking further criticism.

7

Noteworthy Achievements

Narendra Modi, India's 14th Prime Minister, has left an indelible mark on the nation and the world through his remarkable achievements and unwavering dedication. From rising through the ranks of Indian politics to spearheading transformative initiatives, Modi's journey is a testament to his exceptional leadership. His impact is not only measured by his rise to political prominence but also by the numerous accolades, recognitions, and significant milestones he has achieved during his tenure.

Here are the milestones that have defined his legacy, both on the national and international stages, highlighting his role as a pivotal figure in shaping India's trajectory in the 21st century.

1. Modi appeared on the cover of Time Magazine twice, in March 2012 and June 2014.

2. He received the Indian of the Year award from CNN-IBN in 2014.

4. Time Magazine listed him among the 100 most influential people in the world.

5. Forbes ranked him as the 15th most powerful person globally in 2014, rising to 9th place in 2015.

6. Bloomberg Market Magazine recognised him as the 13th most influential person in the world in 2015.

7. In 2021, he earned the title of a "Pivotal Leader," alongside Jawaharlal Nehru and Indira Gandhi, who profoundly influenced Indian politics.

8. Fortune Magazine's 2015 edition acknowledged him as one of the world's greatest leaders.

9. Numerous surveys consistently ranked Modi as one of the top three global leaders.

10. A statue of Narendra Modi was unveiled at Madame Tussauds Wax Museum in London to commemorate his achievements.

12. Modi became the second most followed politician on social media platforms like Facebook and X.

13. In 2018, he was the third most followed world leader on X and the most followed on Instagram and Facebook.

14. He received the United Nations' highest environmental award, the "Champion of the Earth," in 2018.

15. The International Solar Alliance honoured him for advancing solar energy.

16. Modi was awarded the Seoul Peace Prize in 2018 for his efforts in fostering international cooperation, promoting economic growth, and advancing human development.

17. His image was displayed on the ADNOC building in Abu Dhabi during his second term as Prime Minister.

18. At an event held by the Texas India Forum in Houston, Modi received the "Key to the City of Houston from Mayor Sylvester Turner. The event was attended by over 50,000 people and prominent American political leaders, including then-President Donald Trump.

19. The Bill and Melinda Gates Foundation honoured Modi with the Global Goalkeeper Award in New York in 2019 for his contributions to safe sanitation in India.

20. Modi's efforts in elevating India-US relations led to him being awarded the Legion of Merit by former President Donald Trump.

21. He, along with then-Prime Minister of Australia, Scott Morrison, and former Prime Minister of Japan Shinzo Abe, was honoured as an "Original Architect" of the QUAD (Quadrilateral Security Dialogue) alliance, all receiving the Legion of Merit award.

22. The world's largest cricket stadium in Ahmedabad was renamed the Narendra Modi Stadium on February 24, 2021, in tribute to him.

State Honours

Besides receiving numerous prestigious awards and widespread public appreciation, Modi also garnered awards and honours from various countries across the world. Here is a list of the top honours bestowed on him:

Country	Honour	Date	Description
Saudi Arabia	Order of Abdul Aziz Al Saud	3 April 2016	*Special Class*, the highest honour of Saudi Arabia awarded to non-Muslim dignitaries
Afghanistan	State Order of Ghazi Amir Amanullah Khan	4 June 2016	The highest civilian honour of Afghanistan
Palestine	Grand Collar of the State of Palestine	10 February 2018	The highest civilian honour of Palestine
United Arab Emirates	Order of Zayed	4 April 2019	The highest civilian honour of the United Arab Emirates
Russia	Order of St. Andrew	12 April 2019	The highest civilian honour of Russia

Country	Honour	Date	Description
Maldives	Order of the Distinguished Rule of Izzuddin	8 June 2019	The highest honour of the Maldives awarded to foreign dignitaries
Bahrain	King Hamad Order of the Renaissance	24 August 2019	*First Class*, the highest honour of Bahrain awarded to foreign dignitaries
United States	Legion of Merit	21 December 2020	*Chief Commander*, the highest degree of the Legion of Merit
Bhutan	Order of the Dragon King	17 December 2021	*First Class*, The highest civilian honour of Bhutan.
Fiji	Order of Fiji	22 May 2023	*Companion* (CF), the highest civilian honour of Fiji.
Papua New Guinea	Order of Logohu	22 May 2023	*Grand Companion* (GCL), the highest civilian honour of Papua New Guinea.

8

Modi's Famous Quotes

Here are a few inspiring quotes by Narendra Modi that reflect his vision and leadership:

- "Failures should never become a hindrance in the learning process. Instead, we must learn from our failures to strive and overcome challenges in our lives."

- "Each one of us has both; good and evil virtues. Those who decide to focus on the good ones succeed in life."

- "No matter at what speed I move forward, I am never satisfied. If today I run at a speed of 100, I keep an aim of running at 200. World has gone far ahead and we need to match that level."

- "Self-confidence is very important. It's not a pill or herb. There is no tablet that can be consumed for instant confidence. We have to build it every day."

- "You can see the change you want to, be what you want to be."

- "India does not need to become anything else. India must become only India. This is a country that once upon a time was called the golden bird."

- "People's blessings give you the power to work tirelessly. The only thing required is a commitment."

- "The world has crafted a beautiful balance of collective action - common but differentiated responsibility and respective capabilities."

- "Knowledge is limited to things that you are already familiar with. But creativity takes you further than knowledge onto a larger canvas. Creativity can take you to new areas where nobody else has ventured before."

- "Hard work never brings fatigue. It brings satisfaction."

- "We walk together, we move together, we think together, we resolve together, and together we take this country forward."

9

Learning from Modi's Life

At the heart of Narendra Modi's life are the enduring values and principles that have forged his extraordinary path to leadership. His rise from modest beginnings to the highest office in India underscores the transformative power of determination and resilience.

Modi's leadership style is characterised by an unwavering commitment to the nation's welfare. His vision for India as a global powerhouse reflects a steadfast dedication to progress and development, emphasising self-reliance and economic growth as catalysts for national advancement.

Throughout his life, Modi has epitomised the belief that leadership should be grounded in serving the people. His ability to connect with individuals from all strata of society highlights the significance of empathy, inclusivity, and a people-centric approach in leadership.

His genuine concern for the welfare of the common citizen and his tireless efforts to uplift the underprivileged underscore the importance of empathy and compassion in leadership. This dedication to serving the people has earned him the moniker *Pradhan Sevak* or Chief Servant.

Furthermore, Modi's commitment to inclusivity and unity is another hallmark of his values. His belief in the idea of *Sabka Saath, Sabka Vikas* (Together with All, Development for All) reflects a vision of an inclusive and harmonious India. This commitment to unity transcends regional, religious, and social divides and emphasizes the value of national cohesion.

The essence of Modi's life story lies in the conviction that authentic leadership transcends the mere acquisition of power. Rather, it hinges on upholding values, principles, and a visionary outlook. His journey serves as a compelling lesson in leadership founded on unwavering integrity, an unswerving commitment to development, and an unyielding resolve to propel India toward a future defined by progress.

In conclusion, Narendra Modi's attitude and values encapsulate the essence of transformative leadership. His unwavering determination, selfless service, and dedication to inclusivity serve as an exemplary model for leaders across the globe. These values not only define his leadership but also offer valuable lessons on how to navigate life's challenges with resilience, empathy, and a commitment to the greater good.

www.ingramcontent.com/pod-product-compliance
Lightning Source LLC
LaVergne TN
LVHW021006200726
843506LV00012B/2183